All Change

For Paddy Bechely
who set me the subjects

and for Sam and Alice
who got on with growing up
while I struggled for the words

look! I can put
" this copy for Liz "
with many thanks
& love
Libby

Coleridge's huuse
17.4.2004

All Change

Poems by Libby Houston

Oxford University Press

Oxford   New York   Toronto

Oxford University Press, Walton Street, Oxford OX2 6DP

Oxford New York Toronto
Delhi Bombay Calcutta Madras Karachi
Kuala Lumpur Singapore Hong Kong Tokyo
Nairobi Dar es Salaam Cape Town
Melbourne Auckland Madrid

and associated companies in
Berlin Ibadan

Oxford is a trade mark of Oxford University Press

© Libby Houston 1993
Illustrated by Peter Melnyczuk

A CIP catalogue record for this book is available
from the British Library

ISBN 0 19 276064 5

Typeset by The TypeFoundry, Northampton
Printed and bound in Great Britain
on acid-free paper by
Biddles Ltd, Guildford and King's Lynn

Contents

Introduction

I began writing poems before I could do joined-up handwriting. I
wrote in a hardbacked exercise book with a chocolate-coloured
cover, 'My Big Book of Songs'. It was in ten parts, written by a
number of my toys. So that, for instance, Part Two was by Gumbo,
my best-loved teddy-bear. Edward and Red Dog shared Part Nine.
Part One belonged to Tangy (which was short for Tangerine), a
donkey. The first poem was:

The different lands.

The Oranges are rustling in the orange tree,
And in the woods are tropical bands.
The Tigers leaping through the trees;
In the Tropical islands.

The donkeys on the Devon Sands
The donkeys by the Sea.
Which country would you rather have?
"Devon for me!"

I suppose it was fair enough for a donkey! For my part, I wanted
more than anything to be an explorer and go to jungles and tropical
islands – I was wondering then if I would be able to get to Africa by
rowing. But maybe I wanted to keep that secret, and kept it secret.
From teachers at any rate.

Or perhaps I wanted it to sound like the poems we copied out at
school, poems that might be about the weather, and often had
questions and answers; poems that were short and always had a
cheerful voice – *lyrical,* I think they would be called. Not the kind of
poem I really liked, the kind I heard at home, which were ballads,
narrative poems, stories – stories of cruel punishments, revenge,
shipwrecks, battles, death and bones, and the grimmer the better . . .
And also nonsense, and jokes.

My brown book is full of cheerful voices, with poems about
flowers and weather, and little dogs as well as donkeys. Sometimes I
got horribly stuck with rhymes, but I made up for that with the
pictures.

Most of the poems in this new book I wrote for radio, so they certainly came in voices; but many different ones. This time there are stories among the songs. Some, like Arachne's or Hanuman's, have been told for hundreds of years and I tell them again, and some are quite new. I have also written about things directly from my own life, and then I have used my own voice without pretending.

I can still get stuck, not with rhymes particularly, just with finding the right words – the best words – all the way through. Something like making up a costume for a fancy dress party: you can't look *exactly* the same as a pea pod, but a row of green balloons would be more like it than a row of red ones; or you'd be nearer the moon with white paint than gold tinsel. I have been stuck for TWELVE YEARS with words that weren't quite good enough before the better ones came! Poems in this book may still change!

And when, at last, I did get to a tropical island – I flew. There I found the oranges on the orange tree (not rustling, but the palm trees rustled). But there were no tigers. No leopards, sloths, tapirs, elephants, anteaters nor antelopes – not so much as a single monkey. Because the island was so far out at sea, animals like that had never been able to reach it. Not by jumping, like Hanuman, not even by swimming. Only some bats, and rats that had stowed away on ships – it was rats that lived in the coconut-trees.

Libby Houston

7

All Change!

All Change! All Change!

When the guard on the train
or when the bus driver
shouts 'All change!'
and everyone has to
grab their things
in a grumbling fluster
and get out again –

just suppose
it was a magician
in disguise
playing a trick,
and in two ticks
all
the shoppers and schoolkids,
mums and dads,
with their papers and cases
and carrier bags,
grandpas, grans,
football fans,
and tourists with their maps
and their tired feet
did change –

and found themselves
out in the street
like a runaway zoo,
with
a bear or two,
a caribou
and a worm, perhaps –
tigers and mice,
a wasp,
a frog,
aardvarks,
ducks
and a kangaroo-dog,

8

a crocodile,
a chimpanzee –
and a few left behind on board,
a sunflower,
a couple of stones
and a
tree –

What do you think you'd be?

Black Dot

a black dot
a jelly tot

a scum-nail
a jiggle-tail

a cool kicker
a sitting slicker

a panting puffer
a fly-snuffer

a high hopper
a belly-flopper

a catalogue
    to make me

          frog

The Dream of the Cabbage Caterpillars

There was no magic spell:
   all of us, sleeping,
dreamt the same dream – a dream
   that's ours for the keeping.

In sunbeam or dripping rain,
   sister by brother
we once roamed with glee
   the leaves that our mother

laid us and left us on,
   browsing our fill
of green cabbage, fresh cabbage,
   thick cabbage, until

in the hammocks we hung
   from the garden wall
came sleep, and the dream
   that changed us all –

we had left our soft bodies,
   the munching, the crawling,
to skim through the clear air
   like white petals falling!

Just so, so we woke –
   so to skip high as towers,
and dip now to sweet fuel
   from trembling bright flowers.

The Dragonfly

There was once a terrible monster
lived in a pond, deep under the water.

Brown as mud he was, in the mud he hid,
among murk of reed-roots, sodden twigs,
with his long hungry belly,
six legs for creeping,
eyes like headlights
awake or sleeping:
but he was not big.

A tiddler came to sneer and jeer
and flaunt his flashing tail –
Ugly old stick-in-the-mud,
couldn't catch a snai-l!
I'm not scared –
when, like a shot,
two pincers nab him, and he's got!

For the monster's jaw hides a clawed stalk
like the arm of a robot, a dinner fork,
that's tucked away cunningly till the last minute –
shoots out – and back with a victim in it!

Days, weeks, months, two years and beyond,
fear of the monster beset the pond;
he lurked, grabbed, grappled, gobbled and grew,
ambushing always somewhere new –

Who saw him last? Does anyone know?
Don't go near the mud! But I must go!
Keep well away from the rushes! But how?
Has anyone seen my sister? Not for a week now –
she's been eaten
for certain!

And then one day, it was June, they all saw him,
he was coming slowly up out of the mud,
they stopped swimming. No one dared
approach, attack. They kept back.

Up a tall reed they saw him climbing
higher and higher, until
he broke the surface, climbing still.

There he stopped, in the wind and the setting sun.
We're safe at last! they cried. *He's gone!*

What became of the monster? Was he ill, was he sad?
Was nobody sorry? Had he crept off to die? Was he mad?

Not one of them saw how, suddenly,
as if an invisible knife had touched his back,
he has split, split completely –
his head split like a lid!

The cage is open. Slowly he comes through,
an emperor, with great eyes burning blue.

He rests then, veils of silver a cloak for him.
Night and the little stars travel the black pond.
And now, first light of the day,
his shining cloak wide wings, a flash, a whirr,
a jewelled helicopter,
he's away!

O fully he had served his time,
shunned and unlovely in the drab slime,
for freedom at the end – for the sky –
dazzling hunter, Dragonfly!

The Story of Arachne

Far in the night the stars shimmer;
   Athene the grey-eyed goddess treads
stairs of stars to a soaring palace
   of golden thrones and silken beds.

Down in the day the children hurry
   here along the lane to Arachne's door –
'She's weaving something special today!'
   They sit quite still round the cottage floor.

Arachne's hands like a dance begin
   drawing her pictures from the bright wool.
'How do you do it? Did the goddess Athene
   teach you herself? It's so beautiful!'

'Teach *me*?' The dance of wool stops dead.
   Her voice falls on them like a stone:
'The goddess Athene I never saw!
   My hands learned weaving on their own!'

'Arachne! Sh – don't talk like that,
   she'd be so angry if she heard you,
you know what happens to people who think
   they're as good as the gods – she'd murder you!'

'Let her hear! Goddess of spinning and weaving –
   but who's ever seen her weave or spin?
Let her come to this house for a weaving match!
   She can do what she likes – if I don't win.'

The words are out. But nothing changes,
   no striding footstep, no voice in the air.
And the day goes by, that day, another.
   But no one forgets Arachne's dare.

How long's she been standing there in the doorway,
    that strange old woman, shaking her head?
'Arachne, my girl,' says she, 'you'd better
    ask pardon of the goddess for what you said.'

'Ask pardon? Old woman, you mind your own business!
    It's her I'm expecting – why doesn't she come?'
In a blaze of gold old age has vanished.
    The stranger's answer strikes her dumb:

'She has come. She is here. I am Athene!
    Ask pardon now, but you'll ask too late.
You dare compete with me – you shall:
    go get your shuttle, and weave your fate!'

No more is said, no rules need making.
    Side by side in the cluttered room
goddess and girl are blind to all
    but the stretching of thread on a wooden loom.

As the hours run, like light on water
   their fingers flicker while rainbows play
round growing tapestries, walls and weavers –
   but who'd dare sit there to watch today?

For grimly and coldly they weave the old stories
   of people punished – or people tricked;
the gods disguised, the gods in triumph:
   picture for picture they match their wits

Till the sun sets. That same moment
   their hands drop. The contest's done!
Weaving as exquisite surely must be equal?
   Or – has Arachne won?

For the goddess trembles as fury fills her –
   or, win or lose, the end's the same:
Arachne's gorgeous cloth she seizes
   and her white hands rip it from the frame.

Like a cry of pain the noise of tearing,
   harsh as she rends it, thread to shred:
she spurns the rags, and with her shuttle
   three times she strikes Arachne's head.

She has gathered a herb from the groves of darkness,
   she sprinkles the girl with its bitter juice.
'You will not die, but you'll learn your lesson –
   I'll put your skill to a different use!'

'We warned you Arachne! Why didn't you listen?'
   They cannot help her, they hear her moan,
she is dwindling down – they stare in horror –
   till she lies at their feet, like a little stone.

Are those her fingers that wove so proudly,
   spread like hairs at her speckled sides?
She will make no sound now. Changed for ever
   she scuttles away to a hole and hides.

Nobody saw the goddess go
    who treads the stairs of the starry dome.
They stand in a huddle, baffled and low –
    but night is falling, they must go home.

Nobody sees, high under the vine-leaves,
    a single thread of silver light
where blessed by the moon a spider spins
    a gift for the world, her web, tonight.

Caterpillar-Keeper

All the willowherb in the yard
went to feed my caterpillar.
Huge and grey, like an elephant's trunk
he was – well, not quite that big.

Here's your breakfast, greedy-guts!
One morning, he just shook his head,
and all that day, and three whole days –
What's wrong? Why won't you eat a bit?
Are you going to die?

Time was, time is and time will be
and my time for eating's finished.
Look closer – as I shake my head
I'm shaking out a silk thread
to make a tent to sleep in.

I look in the jar
and see a brown pellet.
Is he really still alive inside it?

But the insect-book says,
if I only wait,
here, on my shelf, secretly,
a moth is making itself
or being made –
hawkmoth with wings like willowherb,
as pink and green.

I hope it's true – and oh I hope
I'll be just there, and looking,
when his time is right
and he comes walking out!

Something for a Blue-bottle

Some mother or other laid a load of white eggs
    In a rotten bit of food,
And that's how I came into the world –
    And it tasted rich and good!

We had no teeth and we had no legs,
    But we turned the stuff to soup,
And waggled and wallowed and sucked the dregs
    In our maggoty slop-group troupe!

We squirmed in our supper, we twitched in our tea
  Till we could grow no fatter,
Then we all dropped off to sleep – and that was
  The strangest part of the matter,

For we went quite hard and brown, like pods,
  And when it was time to rise,
Blow me if we hadn't been born again
  With wings this time, like – *flies!*

O I'm buzzing and blue and beautiful,
  I'm an ace at picking and stealing!
I've got masses of eyes to see you with
  And legs to run on your ceiling!

What's in the dustbin smelling so rare?
  I'm zooming in to see,
Then I'm coming to dance on your dinner – look sharp,
  You'll find no flies on me.

Talk About Caves

Talk about caves! Tell us,
tell us about them!
What's a cave, what's it like?

'My strongroom, mine,' said the Dragon,
'where I hid my gorgeous gold!'
But he lay gloating there so long,
in the end he turned to stone –
crawl down his twisting throat, you can,
for his breath's quite cold.

'My house once,'
whispered the Caveman's ghost.
'O it was good
wrapped in fur by the fire to hear
the roaring beasts in the wood
and sleep sound in earth's arms!
(If you find my old knife there,
you can keep it)'

'My bolthole from the beginning,'
Night said,
'where I've stayed
safe from my enemy, Day.
I watch through a crack the sun
beating away at the door –
"Open up!" he shouts.
He'll never get in!'

'My home, always,' said Water.
'I wash my hands here
and slow as I like I make
new beds to lie on
in secret rooms
with pillows and curtains
and lovely ornaments,
pillars and plumes,
statues and thrones –
what colours the dark hides!
I shape earth's bones.'

'Don't disturb me,' the Bat said.
'This is where I hang my weary head.'

The Story of Canobie Dick

A tale from the Borders

A bad day at the market for Canobie Dick,
gone there to sell his horses, and no luck:

'Just have to take them home again – and it's late.
Still, there's always the short cut,
west by the hills – '

'The Eildon Hills? I wouldn't! Not
this time of night!'

'Afraid of the fairies, eh?' says Dick,
'I'm not such a fool!'

His two black horses
pick their way up through the gorse
under a pinch of stars, and nothing between but the wind
whirling down Scotland, and him thinking of his empty purse,
when there's a low voice speaks out, right in his path:
Are you selling your horses, man? I'll buy them both.

'Who's there?'

Only a great black rock, crouched like a hare.

'Come on, show yourself! Ghost or devil I don't care,
so long as your money's good!'

The wind's dropped.
A slice of darkness moves out of the dark rock,
and he stares
into the tall shape of a man, what face he has
hidden by a hood –
with a heap of coins held out in a thin hand.

'This is old-fashioned money!'
Dick laughs. 'Where'd you find it?
Looks like it's spent
years in the ground. . .
But it's gold right enough,
I'll take it –
the horses are yours!

I'll need more

Like the creaking of a forgotten
door in a lost house, that voice
that holds him still –

> *If you have more to sell, then bring them*
> *here to me at midnight.*

Says Dick '– I will!'

One night, another –
but where is he taking them?
No house for miles,
it's as if the hill swallows him!
Ghost he may be, but my horses are real –
there's no trace of them!

So the last night Dick says, 'Look,
it's a dreary time and place for buying and selling –
maybe, could I warm myself a while at your dwelling?'

The old man looks at him,
the starlight catching
stars from his hidden eyes.
He sighs:

Very well, if you will.
But I warn you – remember –
if your courage should fail
you'll be sorry for ever.
Follow me then, if you dare.

There's a crack in the rock
dark as death's door.
'That's odd,' says Dick,
'I never noticed it there before?'
The old man steps through,
Dick stumbles behind him
into the earth and down.
Hand and foot feel
a chill tunnel of stone –
You may still turn back,
says the old man, turning.
Says Dick, 'Lead on!'

And then, round a corner,
the walls open, the roof soars,
and a sudden flare
of torches blazing there,
but white, like moonlight, lays bare
a huge hall –
a hall
fit for a palace, buried in the hill!

That's where his horses are!
Stabled each side of it
horse after horse,
every one of them black as water in a deep well –
and as still . . .

But it's not the horses makes him tremble.
Right down the hall runs a stone table,
and sprawled on benches on either side lie
mighty warriors, knights in armour –
coal-black their armour, their matted beards –
heads lolled, mouths gaping,
and not dead:
sleeping.
The air thrums
with the harsh tides of their dreams . . .

And between them,
there, on the table,
nothing for eating,
nothing for drinking,
nothing at all
but a single sword in a scabbard
and a twisted hunting horn.

Run, his heart cries to him, *run!*

He looks round – but the old man's
lifted back his hood
on a face grey as weathered wood
in a stone wall.
Heavy now his words fall:

So it is written:
he who shall sound that horn and draw that sword,
if his heart fail not, he shall be King of Britain.
So speaks the tongue that cannot lie.

King, says Dick, King – me?
I'm thinking long ago
I saw all this in a nightmare –
but what did I do?

What did I do?
What should I do?

But already his feet
are stepping him forward:
he touches the table,
he touches the sword,
he jolts it, it clatters –
only a little,
but a sleeper mutters,
a sleeper stirs with a groan –
Dick grabs the horn!

Shaking like grass
he can scarcely press
its cold little mouth to his own –
King, king – this must be a dream?
He shuts his eyes.
He blows.

Thin as the scream of a rabbit
the cracked note runs round the walls –

And at once in a crash of stone like thunder,
a whinny of wild-eyed horses, all
the warriors leap to their feet with a shout
the length of the hall,
swords drawn, and drawn at him!
And a great voice above the din cries out:

WOE TO THE COWARD THAT EVER HE WAS BORN
WHO DID NOT DRAW THE SWORD BEFORE HE BLEW
THE HORN!

But the rage in the air has snatched him away like paper,
black and white tumbling round him, howling to hurl him
in a whirlwind back through the tunnel, from stone to stone
and out, on to the moor, into the night, alone
where he heard the door in the rock clash closed for ever.

It was there on the dewy grass the shepherds found him
and no more breath beyond this story he told them.

Post-War

In 1943
my father
dropped bombs on the continent

I remember
my mother
talking about bananas
in 1944

when it rained,
creeping alone to the windowsill
I stared up the hill,
watching, watching,
watching without a blink
for the Mighty Bananas
to stride through the Blitz

they came in paper bags
in neighbours' hands
when they came
and took their time
over the coming

and still I don't know
where my father
flying home
took a wrong turning

The Journey of Hanuman, the Monkey who became a God

1 *The Beginning*

In the land of Koshala,
a kingdom in India
once long ago,
in a beautiful city
whose name was Ayodhya –
'not to be fought against',
once long ago
there lived four noble princes.
The eldest and greatest
and mightiest was Rama.

Because of an evil trick
planned by his stepmother
Rama was banished,
cast out of the palace,
the city, the kingdom,
to live in the forest
with the wild beasts and demons
for twice seven years,
clothed in skins like a holy man.

Lakshmana,
closest of brothers,
went with him
to help and defend him;
and Sita, his gentle wife,
bravest of princesses,
stayed by his side
leaving riches and splendour
to share every hardship.
She would not desert him.

Far off in the jungle
they built a rough shelter
from branches and leaves,
where the birds came to Sita
like a gathering of friends –
they ate from her hand,
and to honour her beauty
the peacocks danced her their pavans.

And so more than twelve years passed.

Then, on an ill-starred day,
stepped from the shadows
a strange wondrous fawn,
dappled gold, speckled silver –
'O catch it!' cried Sita,
'to keep for a pet for me!'

Rama gave chase.
But the deer led a long way,
for it was a demon,
to lead him astray.

'Lakshmana, hurry!
I fear something terrible!'

When they got home,
it was so. She had vanished.
They found the hut empty.
They found Sita nowhere.
Not there, and not anywhere –
as if she had dissolved into thin air.

Mountain-path, jungle-path,
noble Lord Rama goes
wretched and desolate
searching for Sita,
heart heavy with grief for her.
It was the Demon-King
ten-headed Ravana
who tricked and kidnapped her –
where did he take her?
But no one knows where.

Sugriva the Monkey-King
promised that he'd find her,
after the monsoon
he sent out his monkey-troops
north and south, east and west –
but there's no sign of her,
not in all India.

High on a slope
running down to the seashore
the monkeys sent south
sat in dismal debate:
'Let's give up and go home.'
'What, go back empty-handed?'
'But we've looked everywhere!'
'Then I vote we just stay here.'
'We'll starve!'
'Yes, we'll starve . . .'
when aroused by the hubbub
old Vulture the Bird-King
stepped out of his mountain-cave,
gave them some news at last:

'Where the sea reaches
the rim of the world
lies the island of Lanka,
home of the Demon-King
ten-headed Ravana.
Last spring I saw him
fly past – in his arms
a young woman was struggling:
that's where he's taken her!
Look for her there!'

The monkey-chiefs cried:
'We can still keep the promise
our king made to Rama!'
Then they looked at the water –
the featureless vastness,
the empty horizon.

'But how can we cross the sea?'
'Who can jump far enough?'
'Who would dare try?'

One monkey sat apart.
His name was Hanuman.
Son of the Wind,
he loved Rama with all his heart.
He'd dare the deed for him.

But he waited without a word
till at last they turned to him:
'Hanuman! No one can jump
half as far as you –
what are you waiting for?'

'That's true!' he cried.
'I'll jump five hundred miles!
Twice as high as the clouds?
I could leapfrog the stars –
for who does things for Rama
finds nothing impossible,
even an ant
could lift up a mountain –

'So,
          stand back,
                    and wish me luck!'

3 *Hanuman Leaps*

This is what happened:

Hanuman
took a deep breath and began
growing bigger
                    and bigger
                              until –
he's like a high cloud, a huge hill!

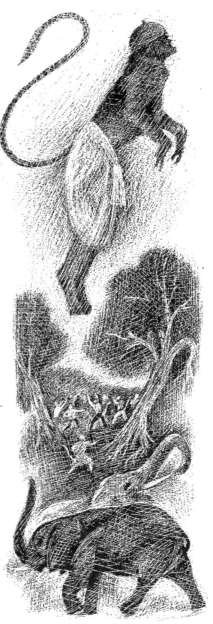

His brown eyes burn
fiercer than twice the sun, he shakes
his hair like a thousand snakes,
the world quakes –
elephants run and hide, trees tumble –
he squeezes the cliffs
till they start to crumble,
gathers his strength
and springs!
Straight as a rocket!
No need of wings –
son of the Wind-God
he leans on the wind.

A million supporters shout and roar
to see him soar.

From heaven's balconies
the bright gods look down too.
They know his task is hard –
will he be brave enough?
They've set a test for him.

Right in his way,
surging up from the deep
comes the mother of all snakes,
the dread Queen of Snakes.
They see Hanuman hesitate.

Wreathing and writhing
she laughs in his face:
'O come, come, tasty mortal,
don't stop, don't hang back,
I'm half-starved for a snack –
and the gods have sent you!
So there's no use disputing it,
now you must enter
my mouth!'

Her jaws gape –
a hundred miles up and down,
and thousands of teeth like a town.

Hanuman
begins growing again,
growing fast, growing vast –
thirty times taller
than Mount Everest –
is that bigger than her at last?
Will it do?

But her huge mouth grows too!

'I give up – you win!'
he shouts, and he leaps in.

But once out of sight,
quick as a wink
Hanuman shrinks
and small as a pin
he nips out again
long before
her terrible jaws
clashing and crunching
have time to shut tight.

Then the Queen of Snakes said:
'Well, you did as I asked.
You did enter my mouth.
You may go on your way now.'

All the bright gods cheered him.

5 *The Friendly Mountain*

Hear the old Sea-God call
down to Mainaka,
the gold-headed Mountain-King
under the water:

'Mainaka! Get ready
to raise your great golden head
out of my restless sea.
Hanuman must be tired –
let him lie down on you.
Everyone's bound to say
how good, how kind we are.'

Hanuman saw the waves
crash and cascade
as the Mountain burst through them:
'What's this? Is the Sea himself
siding against me
to send this eruption?'

The Mountain spoke quickly:
'Great hero, your task is hard –
I'd like to help you! Look,
here's some refreshing fruit –
come and sit down a while,
rest on my head.

'For once, long ago,
all the mountains had wings, you know.
Flew like the birds, we did.
Well, there were some
who got bored flying round like that,
crashed down for fun
on to cities and towns, they did –
squashing them flat.

'So
we were all punished.
The Thunder-God came
and clipped everyone's wings off –
well, all except *mine*, you see.
It was your father, the Wind,
with a mighty gust
blew me to safety here
under the sea,
and I hid from the Thunder-God –
I can still fly!

'So to give you a rest
is the least I can do
to repay your kind father . . .'

But Hanuman never stopped.
'Thanks!' he called back to him.
'Hearing your story's
as good as refreshments.
So don't be offended –
I promised to cross the sea
all in one go
and to rest would be cheating.'

The golden Mainaka
stared crestfallen after him.

'I heard your story too,'
growled the great Thunder-God.
'Still, it was kind of you
offering rest to him.
I'll let you keep your wings.'

6 *Attack from the Deep*

Now the sea laps and leaps,
gallops and glitters
glass-green, or like ink
under Hanuman's shadow –
a whole hundred miles of it
skimming the water.

But down in the depths below,
lurking in ambush,
a blood-hungry demoness
sees him pass over.

Bubbling with glee,
'Monkey-blood! What a dinner!'
she flung her lasso
not at him but his shadow –
and caught it by the tail.

Overhead,
like a dog on a lead,
Hanuman suddenly
felt his speed checked.

He glanced round –
she was right behind,
lunging to grab at him,
grinning and slavering,
mouth like a cave.

Not a moment to lose!
Like a fish
he flicks backwards,
and shrinks in a flash
to the size of a bullet,
he dives through her lion-teeth,
dives for her gullet,
he dives till he reaches
her thundering heart,
and with sharp little fingernails
tears it apart,
tears it in pieces
and tears his way out –
so fast, she never knew what happened.

What a terrible death!
Like a broken-winged aeroplane,
head over heels
goes the grim shadow-catcher,
her cries tumbling after.

Wide are the sea's arms.
She plunges far under.

Then
large and small fishes
bobbed up to thank Hanuman:
'You've sent us food here
to give us good feasts for weeks!'

And the gods dropped down flowers on him.

Huge again, hurrying on
like a thundercloud,
Hanuman sped through the sky
till the sun began
sinking below him now,
red on his right,
when he spied at the sea's edge
a line of grey mountain-tops –

Lanka at last!
The Island of Demons!
The enemy stronghold
where Sita lies captive –

'But how will I know her?
Suppose I don't find her?
And then, if I do –
how on earth can we rescue her?

'Still, I've got this far.
And one thing I do know,
our only hope's me –
so, let's just see what happens . . .'

But he must land secretly,
no one detect him.

The thundercloud vanishes.
Grey in the greying light,
something that might be
a wandering seagull
glides in from the sea.

The palm leaves sway gently
above a good hiding-place.

When the moon rose
and the gold roofs and domes
of the city of Lanka
turned softly to silver,
Hanuman set out
to search every corner
of each room
of every house,
small as a cat now
and quiet as a shadow.

From courtyards to balconies,
doorposts to parapets,
ledges to landings
he bounded and leapt,
till a windowless wall
like a cliff loomed ahead,
and he sprang to the top –
and he stopped.
And he stared.

For there, on the far side,
outshining the moon,
like a cloud charged with lightning –
like a mansion in paradise –
stands Ravana's palace.

Fierce are the monsters
that guard the great gates,
there are guards in the huge halls
and jewel-studded passages,
savage with spears.
But he slips past their feet
like the ghost of a mongoose,
unnoticed, unguessed,
till he reaches the door
of the Demon-King's bedchamber.

Ssh! There lies Ravana –
drunken with wine,
breathing loud as an elephant.
Dark blue his body is,
yellow his shirt,
and on each head
a brilliant crown,
eyes lightly closed –
twenty eyes in a row.

All around him on cushions
lie beautiful women.
They smile in their sleep.

But Sita would never smile,
held here against her will.
Where is he keeping her?

9 *The Secret Garden*

In all that vast labyrinth,
all that great city,
he found not one trace of her.

'Maybe he's killed her?
O how can I go back
without any news of her?
If I tell Rama
I've nothing to tell him,
he'll die of a broken heart.'

Back on the palace wall
Hanuman sat
with his head in his hands

39

when he suddenly noticed
a garden below him,
a garden of fruit-trees,
and under one tree
a small party of she-demons,
yellow eyes glinting
and pointed ears bristling,
brandishing swords and clubs,
jostling and squabbling
round something there
on the ground. . .

Something?

No –
someone!

All sad and forlorn –
like a flower that's been trampled,
like a jewel in the gutter,
like a plank from a shipwreck,
like hope disappointed –
a thin human woman
with eyes black as bees
and the tears pouring
down her cheeks –

Sita!
It must be!

10 *The Search is Over*

Hanuman
hid in the branches
and waited.

The moon set,
the sky paled.
The guards began yawning:
high time to turn in,
and quite safe to leave Sita
alone. She won't run.

By and by, they had gone.

'Lady,' he whispers,
'Look up – I'm your friend!
I bring greetings from Rama!
Your troubles are ending,
for now that I've found you
he'll come here himself
with an army to rescue you.
I'm not a demon-trick –
look, here's his ring!'

Her tears begin shining with joy,
but she cannot speak.

Ten months have come and gone
since she was kidnapped.
Ten months a captive,
refusing to eat or drink,
she is so thin, the ring
slips past her fingers
right down round her wrist.

Hanuman wept.
How could he leave her
to suffer such misery
one moment longer?

41

'O climb on my back,' he said,
'worshipful lady!
I'll carry you home now,
straight home, home to Rama
who grieves night and day for you.'

Sita smiled sadly:
'Bold words, little hero,
when you're not much bigger
than one of my hands.'

'No, wait – you've seen nothing yet!
See me the size I leapt
over the ocean,'
and like a hot air balloon
filling to fly,
he takes shape like a giant –
his head clears the treetops –

'Please stop, I'll believe you!
Please be as you were!

'But I cannot come with you.
Suppose they attacked you?
I'd fall off your back
to the sharks and the crocodiles,
I have no magic.

'Besides, I am Rama's wife.
He, and he only,
should win me away.

'But please tell him to hurry!
For Ravana's sworn
if I keep on refusing
to be his new queen
that he'll cut me in pieces
as soon as the year's gone –
tell Rama I wait for him –
take him this jewel!

'And O, bravest of monkeys,
for you, for the comfort,
the hope, that you've brought me,
I've only my blessings –
but I give you them all:

'May death find no door to you,
fire never scorch you
nor war-weapon harm.
May you safely reach home!'

Bowing low now, his palms
pressed together in reverence,
Hanuman bade her farewell
before springing
aloft through the trees:

'There's just one thing to do still
before I can leave here –
for I came by stealth
unsuspected, unseen,
and I'm not sneaking off again
no one the wiser. No –
this time they'll know me!

'The truth is, I'm starving,
I've not had a scrap,
not a pip, since I landed.
And look at your prison,
an orchard of nectar-fruit –
that's five-star monkey-fuel! . . .

'Don't be alarmed now
whatever you see –
gentle lady, trust me!'

11 *Hanuman's Harvest*

Hark at the panic,
the clamour and hammering
back in the palace:

'Wake up, O King,
there's a monstrous great monkey
gone mad in your garden!'

'A monkey? What's that?
Do you dare to disturb me
with news of a *monkey*?
My guards – what's become of them?
Turned into mice?
They can fetch me some fruit
when they've dealt with this –
monkey!'

'But he's picked all the fruit
and he's picking the trees now,
the guards can't get near him,
he's catching their spears
and he's hurling the trees at them,
worse than a whirlwind –
he's killing us all!'

It was true.

The sweet-scented fruit-groves
lay ravaged and smashed.
Sita's tree stood alone
at the edge of a battlefield,
trees thrown like matchsticks
and demons like broken dolls
flung on the rubbish,
and glorying over it all
like a thunderstorm,
high on the wall
the huge figure of Hanuman

44

blasting the air
with the roar of his war-cry:
'To Rama the Victory!'

Nothing could harm him.

12 *The Demon Champion*

Word reached the King's
mighty son, Indrajita.

He smiled as he armed himself.
This was his secret:
his weapons were magic,
arrows of wondrous power
(some call them *snake-arrows*)
granted him once
by the Lord of Creation.
They coiled round a victim
like rope come alive –
and their ropes were invisible.
None could resist them.

He mounted his chariot
and charged to the battle-front.

Hanuman laughed
when he saw Indrajita,
his bow bright as lightning,
stand poised to take aim at him.

Hanuman laughed
as the arrow flew free.

And then, the next instant,
bound fast hand and foot
and trussed up like a chicken,
he fell to the ground.

'Haul him off to the palace!'
He lay without struggling.

'Suits me all right,' he thinks,
watching their jubilance,
'Now I'll be meeting
King Ravana face to face . . .
find out what we're really up against.'

13 *The King's Rage*

High on his crystal throne
sits red-eyed Ravana,
dazzling with diamonds,
his princes and demon-lords
ranked either side of him.

Hanuman squats on the floor
with his back to him.

'Let Sita go!' he says.
'I come from Rama
and this is his message:
unless you release her now,
death and destruction
and Lanka laid waste
all because of your wickedness.
He's sworn to kill you –
or I would, myself.'

In a trice the chief demon,
each face dark as aubergines,
leaps to his feet roaring:
'Insolent ape!
You can count yourself lucky
the laws of the gods stop me
killing a messenger!
Leave here alive then –
but leave here in shame,

I'll make sure you remember
your visit to Lanka:
Guards!
Set fire to his tail!'

They run to obey,
bringing oil-sodden rags
to wrap Hanuman's tail in
the better for burning,
and mock him and jeer
as they bind it
and wind
it –

But
what kind of monkey
can make his tail
grow?
Like this?
Two hundred miles or –
or is there no end to it?

Three million demons
were needed to hold it down,
all the spare cloth on the island
to wrap it –
'We've used up the last drop of oil
in the palace. . .'

'Bring torches,' the King cried,
'and set it alight!'

Ten laughs laughed Ravana
as the flames flared:
'Take this sizzling scoundrel
and drag him through every street –
let all my citizens
laugh at the spectacle!'

Nobody notices
Hanuman smiling:
'A tour here by daylight
will show me the weak points
where we can attack it.'

And by Sita's blessing
the fire did not hurt him.

14 *The Burning of Lanka*

In no time the city's
set fair for a carnival,
streets thronged with demons
of all forms and features,
to see the procession.

And look, here it comes!
First the dancers and acrobats,
trumpets and drums – and now,
what you've been waiting for,
Hanuman!

'Look at him!'
'Big as a 'ouse – '
' – if you pricked him, he'd burst.'
'Just an oversize monkey!'
'He's harmless.' 'He's helpless –
we've got him in chains.'
'That's his *tail* – feel the heat!'
'That'll teach him.' 'Keep back!'
'Will we see any fireworks?'

'Have fun,' he says quietly,
and nobody hears.
'Soon enough you'll be crying
because of your king.'

48

And suddenly,
just where he was,
in the midst of them,
Hanuman shrank.

The chains simply fell from him.

Somebody screams.
Where's he gone?
Like a rat, like a
runaway sparkler
he dodges and darts
till he reaches a pillar
and so to the rooftops –
'Up there!'
Someone's spotted him –

Where?
But he's growing,
he's growing gigantic,
and now they can all see him,
proud as a ringmaster,
lashing his tail –
how the flames stream and billow
and flicker and fly! –
in a firework display
that fills them with horror and dismay:

For off he goes
capering over the housetops,
the touch of his tail
like a match to a fuse
or a birthday-cake candle,
for each way he turns –
like a comet gone crazy –
the gold roofs of Lanka
go up in a blaze.

And then, with a terrible howl,
the crowds scatter.
They run for their lives,
they dive under the water.
And loud though the flames roar,
his voice rings the louder:
'To Rama the Victory!
I am his servant and messenger
Hanuman,
Son of the Wind!'

Behind them, their city
burns down to the ground.

15 *A Rest by the Sea*

Hanuman gazed
at the smouldering ruins:

'Ravana thinks
he can do what he likes,
for the gods cannot stop him.

'But monkeys and men can,
and if he's forgotten –
well, that should remind him.'

He sat at the sea's edge
and let the low ripples
close over his tail,
and his thoughts drifted free
through the many strange scenes
that had brought him to Sita –

To Sita!

To Sita
alone in the garden!

'O what have I done?
In my anger and rage
I forgot all about her!
That's just like a monkey,
a cursed, careless monkey!
She must have been burned –
the whole city was burned.
Did I come here to find her
to kill her? And with her,
the hopes of all those
I love best in the world?

'O that's far worse than Ravana!
What can I do?
I'll jump straight in the water
and let the sharks finish me!'

'Be of good cheer!'
called the bright gods
with urgency –
'Sita is unharmed,
her goodness and faithfulness
cannot be burned.
The Fire-God is her friend.'

16 *Home*

Then there's no more to do
but get home swift and sure now,
with news full of danger
but the news Rama longs for.

The pearl Sita gave him
like a lamp on his forehead,
Hanuman made with all speed
for the mountain-tops,
marking the highest
his springboard for home –
though his heart was back
long before.

Now, at the summit,
the gusts of his breath
blowing hard as a blizzard,
he braces himself
on the brink of the sky
like a long-distance diver –
and lets fly!

Far behind fades the thunder
of landslide and avalanche.
Longing and eagerness
carry him right through
the bounds of the atmosphere,
on into space –

When he looked down, he faltered:
a pattern of patches
lay spread like a banquet:
'Those islands weren't there
in the sea I crossed yesterday!
Have I come the wrong way?'

But the islands were clouds,
for the sky was beneath him now,
what he thought water
the shimmer of moonlight
with, here and there glinting like fishes,
the stars.

High on a slope
running down to the seashore,
the monkeys sent south
sit there watching and still
like a hill of old treestumps –
they've not moved a muscle,
not spoken nor slept
since their champion vanished,
a speck in the distance.

At first imperceptibly –
sensed before heard,
like a ranging mosquito –
the sky begins humming,
a hum that homes in over the sea
to roar like a huge wave
above, around, on all sides,
suddenly wringing their ears
in a shrill shriek –

They leap to their feet
squinting up, staring wildly,
in time to see Hanuman
hurtle to touch-down.

He bounds to their open arms,
mission accomplished.

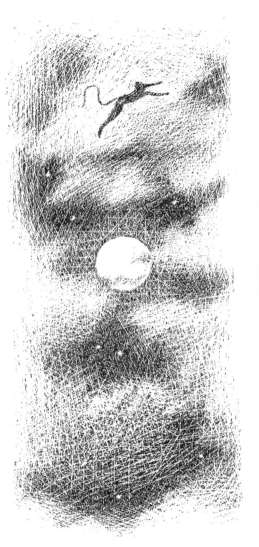

17 *And Then*

So ends the story
of Hanuman's journey.

But what about Sita?
Did Rama rescue her?
What happened next?

Well, the monkeys themselves
built a causeway of rocks and stones
over the sea
to the Island of Demons,
and Rama, borne high
on the shoulders of Hanuman,
led them to war.

Bitter and long
was the Battle of Lanka
with stories enough there
to fill a whole book
for another day's telling.

But though they were strong
and their weapons the deadlier,
one by one
Ravana's warriors
fell
till at last
none was left
but the ten-headed king himself.

Out through the gates of the city
charged Ravana,
blazoned with wrath
in his radiant gold chariot.
'This is the day I send Rama,'
he roared,
'to the King of the Dead!'

It was Rama's last arrow
that slew him and laid him low.

Far across heaven
the bright gods rejoiced
crying 'Victory! Victory!'

Heartsick and weary
the demons surrendered,
their new king no enemy.
Sita was found safe and sound.
It was over.

Then haloed with happiness
Rama and Sita came
home, home across the sea,
home to Koshala
their long exile over,
from fourteen years' banishment
home to Ayodhya.

There with due splendour
they were crowned King and Queen.

18 *Hanuman's Gift*

Long were the glad days
of friendship and feasting
until, as it must,
came the moment for leaving,
and laden with good gifts
the monkeys went home.

But when Hanuman
knelt down before him,
King Rama said:
'Prince among monkeys,
what gift can we give you
to match what you've done for us?'

Hanuman said:
'I would serve you for ever.
Your name's on my heart,
every bone of my body.

'And this is my wish,
that so long as your name
shall be spoken on earth,
just so long may I live, Lord,
so long may I hear it.'

'So be it!' said Rama.
'And as long as the world lasts
may sickness and old age
with death keep their distance.'

Then Sita leant down,
and her own shining necklace
of pearls bright as moonbeams
she placed round his neck:

'Dear Hanuman,
no man or woman was ever
so brave or so daring,
so faithful and true.
Immortal you shall be,
and, one with the gods,
may the gods themselves honour you!'

And so it was.

Hanuman became the Monkey God.

A Rhyme for Autumn

Go and catch a falling leaf
  Before it comes to rest,
For every leaf's a lucky day
  And lucky days are best.

Another Rhyme for Autumn

Try and catch a falling leaf
  Before it hits the deck –
A lucky day? More likely several
  Strange knots in your neck.

The Tale of the Estuary and the Hedge

'Come,' said the small slimy
estuary pleasantly,
'come!' to the hedge that guarded
the door of the low-lying meadow.

'Follow me along my easy
course,' smiled the mud. 'Oh
your butter won't turn,
your daisies won't run!
I assure you, you won't be away for long.'

Doubtful, the hedge packed
its hawthorn blooms, sparrow nests
and ditchweeds neatly in a bundle,
to follow – with a guilty look behind:
Had the meadow noticed?

Hour on hour lazily
the little estuary
crept and curved,
the hedge trotting after.

The air became brighter,
new the birds that swam
or perched momentarily,
net-heaps ousting ploughs
and the estuary gaining in girth.

Now, like an ambush
round the corner, the land
stops! The hedge is lost!

'It is The Sea – it is only
the sea,' smiles on the estuary.
'Don't be yellow-hearted! Come,
follow,
      I'll
         be
            leading
          you . . .'

Outside In

    the window keeps on
      banging but I'm
      not going to look

Ant Town

Ants live in mazes, not houses.
I lifted the roof of their town:
hundreds of thin black legs
scurrying up and down
black cracks in the brown clay,
some carrying long white eggs.
How can they know their way?
Even the eggs must be black
when I put the stone back.

In the Bee-Factory

It is night in the factory
where bees make bees,
always night and little sleep,
all the long hot summer through.

All the long dark summer through,
cradle-builders
are steadily fixing
wax to wax
for the Great Queen follows them,
stepping from rim to rim to drop
the right egg in the right cot –
she must not stop,
she cannot stop –
ten thousand cradles for making bees!

Back down the line
eggs begin hatching,
hungry grubs rising,
night-nurse bees bustling
with bee-milk to feed them,
worker-babies
to work for the factory.

Fat little grubs grow,
shed their skins,
grow again
(up the line now, new
eggs begin hatching)
till they reach the right size,
turn, and close their eyes –

Here lies the secret,
the pride of our factory!
Go to sleep maggot –
wake all bee!
Shiny legs, glossy wings,
striped backs, stings –

Success every time!
Thousands the same!
Fresh for the work ahead –
hard work till they're dead!

And what's the work?
Out in the brightness! Look,
up from the factory gate they rise
into a haze of sun and colour,
tastes to trace, sisters to tell –
their job's the sweetest
flowers to search for

to gather the pollen,
and the nectar for honey,
to feed the dark factory
where bees make bees
to fly in the brightness
gathering pollen,
and nectar for honey,
to feed the dark factory
and make
bees

Flying to India

And so we climbed inside the plane,
Sam, Alice and I,
to sit in the sky – to fly
all the way over the side of the world
to India
was our adventure.

FASTEN YOUR SEAT BELTS!
They fastened the door,
the engines behind us,
the runway before,
and, lurching gently, we
started to creep
as low as a moth
on the kitchen floor
to wait our turn
where, large and small,
like apparatus-day
in a giant machines' school hall,
the aeroplanes queue
for the take-off run
one by one . . .

The Jumbo's gone –
and now it's us!
Like a boiling kettle
at the whistle
the engines screaming,
we're off! We're running
the wide white road
like a galloping horse
the last fence ahead,
faster and faster,
so heavy inside
you could feel her gather up
all of her power

to hurl her metal
and all her load
clumsy and loud
at the thin light air –
nothing can stop us!
Up goes the nose
and the people in front of us
tilting backwards
nearly on top of us,
things bump and jolt –
and through the window,
look, there's a roof,
and Windsor Castle!

Magical racehorse, horse of metal,
far did your proud jump go!

They brought us strange food,
black-haired ladies
in blood-red blouses,
with smiling faces,
and tiny paper packets of pepper,
salt, milk powder, toothpicks and sugar –
we picked and poked, we sprinkled and stirred,
and ate,
and drank:
enchanted food
it might have been
for we saw what we had never seen.

For when I looked out,
I saw the sea
stretch like a fan,
edging the land
far, far below, and nothing between –
I saw England's roots, pale roots of sand
going down deep through the rich blue water,

and all the waves between England and France
so long and still
you could count them all.

Suddenly we bucked and stumbled –
I was scared, I thought aeroplanes never trembled.
       What's happened?
A wisp like a ghost brushed by –
            it was just a bump in the road of the sky!
   Thick air and thin, air rising and falling:
            strange road,
                      made of so much nothing!

              Overhead
          it was brilliant blue,
            but under us now
         there began to gather
     a fat froth, milky and thick, until
            we were cut off
with an endless carpet of candy-floss
              to cross
          alone and small –
like a lonely fly upstairs in an empty hall.
     Then we dipped through.

Down through the ceiling we came, to a land
where tiny square houses stood neat in a row
no bigger than dolls' houses for dolls,
                by a road like a ruler,
          and coming and going,
matchbox lorries, pin-men's cars,
            none of them knowing
                  that we could see!
We stopped for breath, it was Germany.

Night poured round us
and on we went,
in black, to Rome,
where the floor was swept.
The engines hurt, they roared at our ears so loud –
and at last we slept.

Somewhere behind us, far away,
our street lay
tucked in that shadow-bed
of night –
but though the dark held on to our tail,
we ran ahead,
ran, till we overtook time, meeting the next day
half-way, straight for the sun's big apricot,
and first for us the golden light,
showing the way!

O we were flying above a brown country:
brown rocks, brown sand, and not a tree
or field or town that we could see,
but a thin road, going on and on
through the dreary deserts of Iran.
We grew weary, bored, tired,
sitting so long
stuck in the air –
How much longer till we get there?

Deserts and mountains passed,
and then, at last,
the world spread open a vast
yellowy green and blue check table-cloth,
bunches of villages set among the squares,
and the pilot, his voice all fuzzy,
announced where we were:
it was India!

Lovely were the clouds
the day put up like flags to greet us,
twists of cream or barley-sugar,
curly locks of hair –
it was dinner-time; we were nearly there . . .

Now over fields with wavy edges
and felt-penned hills with furry faces
under a cloud like a scarf we flew,
it was brown beneath white beneath blue –
when suddenly, higher than us, one after
another, above the cloud we saw, like
planets unknown to the world below,
dazzling black rocks and bright snow –
peaks of the giant Himalayas
shining, as if they'd come out to see us!

This was the land our ticket promised,
we came in to land –
our friends were there to meet us –
Look! There's Chris and Moraig and Hamish!
We touched the ground,
we laughed and shouted and ran
in the fresh wind and the warm sun!

Empty,
forgotten,
the magical horse lay dumb.

Rotting Song

old green cheese
old green cheese,
you'll never get another chance –

Green cheese sits in the airtight tin
wondering just how those mites got in,
crosses off the minutes to the sinking knife –
hasn't found out he's in prison for life

Cold meat sweats on the larder plate,
a wet flesh target, doesn't have to wait,
in dive the blue flies, drop their eggs –
drive him crazy those hairy legs

Dud plum squashed on the kitchen floor
can't see what he's been put there for,
knows he's going soft but he can't stir –
old age buries him deep in fur

Dud plum, cold meat, old green cheese
rot in your own time at your ease,
nobody minds, nobody cares –
moved out their lives and gone downstairs

Midsummer Stars

A long time coming.
When the dark was complete

when they knew it was safe
they opened out like daisies:

twisted and faint the dragon
and stretched in flight the swan

brightest of all the high harp
slung between them

The Ballad of the Great Bear

When Zeus was king of the gods
   and Hera was queen,
There was a land called Arcady
   of wild woods and green.

And nymphs played in the deep glades
   where few strangers came.
The fairest nymph in Arcady,
   Kallisto was her name.

One day, and she was hunting,
   Zeus saw her there,
And he loved her for her bold step
   and the white ribbon in her hair.

Queen Hera paced the cold halls.
   Cruel was her frown.
'My husband gone with a wood-nymph –
   and now she's borne him a son!

'And she be unpunished?
   This day I'll go
and pay her a visit in Arcady –
   and no mercy show!'

In the deep woods she found her.
   She threw her to the ground.
'Say good-bye to your beauty, girl!'
   'Mercy!' Kallisto moaned.

But her skin began prickling
   with hairs thick as grass.
She saw her hands curved round
   into crooked claws.

Now she begged *Mercy*
   a growl grazed the air
From a mouth become gaping jaws –
   the jaws of a bear.

A great bear roams Arcady,
   the long years roll by.
Nothing but fear and loneliness
   to keep her company.

One day a boy came hunting,
   his spear still untried.
'Now winter's in the air, I need
   a good bear-hide.'

The bear stood gazing at his face.
   A strange growl he heard.
It's your son! her eyes told her.
   She could not say a word.

Zeus glanced from his high tower.
    Then pity felt he.
'The boy kill his mother – No,
    this must not be!'

He spun the air about them
    to a whirlwind wild.
Far up through the sky it carried
    mother and child.

In the dark depths of space glimmered
    one star's bright bead
When a swarm of lights sprang up beside,
    like scattered seed.

Nightlong over Arcady
    their pale fires burned.
Unchanging in their pattern
    they turned as the world turned.

Then, now – for ever,
    while earth's seasons run –
Still their slow circle tread
    the Great Bear, and her son.

Orion the Hunter

Here comes a stranger to the woods.
Strong he looks, handsome as a god.
Listen to him shout:

'Orion I am! Orion the Hunter!
Wild beasts of the world, beware!

'Old boar, do you hear?
Your fierce tusks frighten me –
like icicles on a little twig!
Roar will you, lion?
I'll roar your stuffing out
till you're flat as a rug!
Big shaggy bear,
you'd better hug yourself
when I set foot on your track!
Hide? I'll have your hides, every one –
                    for I am
                              Orion!'

Running lightly through the morning
bound for hunting with her bow,
Artemis the huntress goddess
heard his boasting, bold as a bell.

'Hunt with me,' she called, 'Orion!
Mightiest in all the forest!
You and I should have good hunting –
come and join me in the chase!'

What danger and delight each day
they shared – until her brother heard,
her brother the sun-god, great Apollo:

'Can my sister really think
this boasting bumpkin, this mere man,
fit to hunt beside a goddess?
Time I stopped it – time I cut him
well and truly down to size.'

And off he went to Mother Earth,
mother of all wild animals.
She listened to his plan with pleasure.

So, as he asked, from soil and stone
she made a giant scorpion
with claws already poised to grab
and grip like pincers, arching tail
to jab its deadly sting, and sides
as tough as steel. 'Now look!' she said.

Like a relentless dinosaur
or huge machine it lurched to life.
She wiped her hands, and shook
                                    with laughter.

Striding boldly through the morning
bound for hunting with his bow,
Orion felt the forest shudder,
first a tremor, then a roar,
a crashing crumbling rending grinding
thundering through the wood behind,
and whirling round, he found the monster
close upon him, set to strike.

He drew his bow – but all his arrows
glanced and fell like bits of straw.
Head-down he ran between the pincers,
plunged his sword with all his power.
It broke in pieces in his hand.
He might as well have stabbed a rock.

Orion knew then that some god
was angry with him, meant him dead.
He flung his weapons down, and fled.

Far below him stretched the sea.
A steep path, much too steep and narrow
for the scorpion to follow,
led to the shore. He scrambled down.
The waves came up like friendly hands
offering rescue. In he leapt,
and swam, and never once looked back.

Apollo, watching from the cliff-top,
called his sister: 'Artemis, quick!
Here's a chance to try your skill –

'See that black dot in the water
heading out to sea? I tell you
that's a cruel and ruthless robber
who's just smashed and stripped your temple!
Will you let him get away?
You could still stop him, with an arrow – '

Artemis, white-lipped with fury,
picked an arrow, drew the bow,
let fly.
            'Good shot – I knew you could!'
her brother cried. She smiled, and dived
straight from the cliff to claim her victim.

Where the waves were red she found him
floating still – no ruthless ruffian
but her own beloved Orion.
Cruel the trick, too cruel to speak.

Slowly she brought him in to shore
and wept there till the night crept down
and gently covered him with darkness.

Then she took his lifeless body,
stepping through space to mount the stairs
the stars made for her, and on heaven's
heights at last, star-changed, she set him
till the world's end the world's champion,
with sword and club as he once stood
to face the wild beasts in the wood.

But to show how he was driven
to his death, she hurled the scorpion
out to the far side of the night.
So, as the stars wheel, when Orion
sinks from sight the monster rises,
fixed in a chase that cannot reach him
nor with its dimmer stars outshine him.

And every year when days begin
to shrink, and darkness wells with winter,
back to our sky he comes again
like a loyal friend – O welcome him,

                        Orion the Hunter!

For the Record

glancing away

saw for a second
neck and neck with us
on the motorway
some vole
going like one fur
cylinder –

no chance!

falling back fast
pulled out of it
shot off for its
own slow lane
through the briar –
like a star

Centrifugalized in Finsbury Park

Hey I just had a go on one of them
things! Didn't notice it had a name,
but anyone could see what it was going to do to you –

something like a giant-size round biscuit-tin without a lid
made of wire-netting, and all around the inside,
niches, like for statues, 30 or so, like coffins, only
upright, and open of course with the kind of lattice –
with a padded red heart at head-height.

74

Paid the money, got myself a niche, and stood and waited
with a little chain dangling across my hips,
until it was full, the gate shut, the music started
and the thing began to whirl.

It wasn't the stomach, it was what to do with the head:
no good looking down, but if you let your head back
it felt as if it was going to go on going back, or off –
a bit peculiar, shut my eyes to get through that.

And as it whirled, the whole thing turned on end,
more or less vertical – well, I'd seen that right from
the park gates and couldn't believe it, which was why –
and opening my eyes again then, just found myself
lying there – lying down face up, lying up face down
over the whole fairground!

And it didn't make you scream like the top of the Big
Wheel, but smile – look up and everyone else is standing there,
hanging there, smiling, look down and you might as well be a lazy
bird on the wind, though I did forget I could let go,

and the only strange feeling was,
every time you were on the down side hurtling up again,
you left the skin of your face behind for a second.
You know I've never dared try anything quite like that
before, and it was just very nice!

And when it slowed down and sank down, and all of us
were ordinary upright, and unhitched our little chains,
I only staggered a couple of times, disappearing
on ground level into the dark – and nobody was sick.

Like a Maze

One day, just after Christmas, we went to the Sales.
My sister wanted a dark blue tracksuit,
my mum was going for vests and curtains,
coats for us, boots – next year's presents!
And anything good, she said, going cheap at the big store.

We pushed in through the glass door.

'Follow us, now. Don't get lost.'
Follow-my-leader, my
mum's red coat led
twist and turn through a jostling jungle
of coats, arms, bags, backs, thick and thin,
deeper and deeper in –

And then she stopped.
She reached in a tray.
I looked away –
and there through a gap, just for a moment,
I saw a row of little fur dogs on a table,
and one of them yapped,
flapping its red tongue!
And there was Paddington with his sou'wester!

When I looked back –
they'd gone,
my sister and mum!

Which way? I couldn't
tell, I couldn't
see a way at all, I couldn't
go straight ahead, there was
no straight ahead, for the
cases and counters I
couldn't see over and
couldn't see round and the
hedges of blouses and

bushes of skirts,
clumps of trousers,
fences of packets of
shirts, and suddenly
mirrors
headed me this way and that till I couldn't
remember where I'd been,
and people in all the space between
I didn't know, I'd never seen!

I came to a dead-end walled in mouthing tellies.

There was the lift! I got in – *Going up,*
said a voice, and I couldn't get out,
a fat shiny shopping bag jammed me back,
a woolly elbow caught my hat –
I saw a red coat – 'Mum!'

The wrong face looked down.

The lift stopped. Quick!
But the river of people swept me
out like a stick
into the glaring halls again,
just the same and not the same,
I didn't know where I was, or where I was
going, and people stepped into me, knocked me
as though I was nothing
and not there at all –

Then I came to a barricade
of criss-crossed racquets
with a dark lane beyond
lined with jewels, like a king's hoard,
and bright at the end I found
a room like a secret nobody knew –
like me.
I stood at the door.

Silver and gold it was, with walls
of glass where tall white dresses shone
as still as snow.
Nobody was there
but brides, they were statues,
white flowers in their hair,
smiling up at the air,
and a green chair,
arms wide,
waiting –
all waiting.
I stepped in.

The curtain like a veil flew back –
a towering lady, all in black,
came striding out!

She was looking down, with a frown
like hooks, her mouth a red
stitch pulled tight,
her thin heels
pounced on the carpet
like sewing needles
coming straight for me –
I froze. She saw me. Her
eyes were on me, she
opened her mouth –
                          and I ran!

I bumped and crashed, I couldn't see,
I tripped on the roots of a silver tree,
a flurry of hats flung down with me –
I hurt my knee.

Somebody picked me up, somebody gave me a sweet,
somebody took my hand and led me to a seat.
And after a while, my mum and sister
came rushing up, looking worried and flustered
and cross. My mum said,
'Well! I'm not bringing you again!'

They hadn't bought a thing!

The Key to the Maze

Is it the maze you're going to?
Here is the key to take you through:
whenever the path divides in two,
keep to the right.

                    Is that right? Is it true?

I don't know. But somebody said so.

79

Tam Lin

Don't go down to Carterhaugh,
*   Carterhaugh, Carterhaugh,*
if you go to Carterhaugh,
*   Tam Lin'll get you!*
If you go to Carterhaugh,
*   Tam Lin'll get you!*

Janet sits in her high window
    looking out over her father's lands,
a thread of gold in her yellow hair,
    a threaded needle in her hand.

'Oh I'm tired of these grey castle walls!
    And I'm tired of sewing seams!
I'd rather be down in Carterhaugh
    among the leaves so green!'

She has thrown her sewing on the chair,
she's plaited up her yellow hair,
gathered her skirts of green so fair,
run lightly down the castle stair,
    and she's away to Carterhaugh
with a laugh at her own daring.

The wood was quivering with the hum of bees
and no one she saw
but a milk-white horse stood under the trees
and roses, red and white, in a tangle of briar
'Some for my room, one for my hair – '
two she has picked and reaching her hand for three –
he's there,
sprung up behind her out of thin air
saying: 'Lady, you'll pick no more!

'Who said you could pick my roses, Janet,
or the green branch you've broken?
How came you here to Carterhaugh
without my permission?'

'Permission from you sir? I like that!
Just who may you be?
I'll come and go as I please here –
this wood belongs to me!'

Tam Lin was no wild robber,
he wasn't rough or grim,
but there was a strange light in his face,
nine silver bells about his waist,
for he was a knight of Elfland
that served the Fairy Queen.
And not her gold but her love he stole
and was gone, like a dream.

'What's come over Janet these days?
She's changed.
She won't play chess, she won't come dancing.'
'I've heard her crying in her room!'
'She went to Carterhaugh. She did.' 'Did she?'
'You ask her – go on.'

'O go away! Mind your own business!
Just leave me alone!'

Her father's coming up the stair:
   'Something's wrong now, tell me Janet,
are you in trouble? Is it a man?'
   'Father, it's true, I won't deny it –

'If he were human flesh and blood
   a better man you'd never see –
but my lover is a knight of Elfland,
   he won't, he cannot marry me!

'O but the milk-white horse he rides
   goes lighter than the wind,
shod with silver shoes before,
   and gold shoes behind – '

She has brushed aside her tangled hair,
she's taken her cloak of green so rare,
she has left her father standing there,
run wildly down the castle stair,
   and she's away to Carterhaugh
with her eyes red from weeping.

The wood was shivering with the fall of leaves
       and no one she saw
but a milk-white horse stood under the trees
and a few last blooms withered on the briar.
   'Will this bring him back? Is he here?'
Two she has picked and reaching her hand for three –
       he's there,
   sprung up beside her out of thin air
   saying: 'Lady, you'll pick no more.

'Why are you picking the dead flowers, Janet,
   the dead leaves from the vine?
And would you harm the unborn baby
   that's your child and mine?'

'O tell me, Tam Lin, tell me,
 if you love me at all,
is it true you're from the other world?
Were you never christened in a church?
 O aren't you real?'

Tam Lin took her by the hand
 and all the woods grew dim.
'I was born as human a child as you were.
Roxburgh was my grandfather
 and I used to ride with him.

'We rode out to hunt the red deer
 with no luck, that day.
Bitter and sharp the wind got up.
 I lost my way.
My horse stumbled on something,
 threw me to the ground,
and so strange a sleep came over me
 I couldn't move or make a sound
but I could see a tall woman standing there
 as I lay so still:
the Queen of Elfland, come for me,
 to her palace under the hill.

'O Elfland's a fine place to live,
 many stories I could tell,
but at the end of every seven years
 they must give a payment to Hell,
and they pay with one of their people
 in the fires of Hell to burn,
and because I was once a human lad,
because I'm made of flesh and blood,
 I fear it's my turn.

'But you, if you will, can save me,
    for all their might
has no power as strong as a true heart –
    but it must be tonight!'

'Tonight? Why's that?' says Janet.
    'And what are you asking me?'
'To stand in the eye of a nightmare
    to set me free.

'For this is the night of Hallowe'en
    when the fairy people ride
through England, through Scotland,
    through the whole world wide –
you must wait for us at Miles Cross
    on the bare hillside.

'Wait for us there at the dead hour
    between twelve hours and one,
bring holy water from the church with you,
    you'll take no harm,
cast it in a circle around your feet
    and wait there, alone.'

    'And if I do,
out in the dark among all the weird riders
    how will I ever know which one is you?'

'You'll see a black horse, let it by,
    and after that, a brown –
then quickly run to the milk-white steed
    and pull the rider down,
for I ride on the milk-white steed,
my right hand gloved, the other bare,
    and a gold star on my crown.

'Then hold tight, hold on, hold me fast,
loose your hands once and I'm lost,
they'll fight for me with all their powers,
change me to wild beasts in your arms
    to make you let go.
Only remember, whatever you hold
is me, the father of your child,
is me, to be your heart's desire,
is me, and I would never hurt you –
    believe it so!

    'And last of all
they'll change me into a burning coal
    with flames in your hand:
throw it in the water, love,
    and I'll come out a man,
wrap me then in your green cloak
    and tomorrow we'll be wed –

'Now I'm away, they must not see us –
    O Janet, don't be afraid!'

Supper's cleared and the lights grow lower,
the shadows twitch and gather and glower,
the corners rustle, the girls are scary:
    'Coming up to bed now, Janet?'
    'The wind's sharp as knives!'
'O it's a bad night Hallowe'en,
    I can't bear the stories.'
'Last year remember the ghost on the step?'
'You please yourself Janet,
    I'm not staying up.
    Goodnight.'

'Goodnight.'

She has looked in the mirror and said a prayer,
she has crumpled her bed like a body there,
fastened her cloak of green so rare,
slipped quietly down the castle stair,
   and she's run off to Miles Cross
with her mouth tight from trembling.

At the dark crossroads all by herself she stands
for the dead of night to call up the cavalcade.
She has sprinkled the holy water with a cold hand,
no moon or star on her, but the black wind like a blade.

   What was that now? Where?
   A strange noise jangles on the air,
   growing louder, coming nearer,
   horses' hooves and horses' bridles,
   and over the brow of the hill a pale
long procession towards her of all the fairy riders.

There's a black horse passes her, so close,
   passing, and gone, and now a brown –
and there's a white horse, the white horse, his horse, now!
She has grabbed the rider by the foot
   and pulled him down.

Tam Lin's away! Tam Lin's away!

Is it black night or blinding light?
And what is it held in her shaking hands?
Something hissing, with gleaming fangs –
a twisting snake, a spotted snake –
   'I must hold on, he said, he said.'

What must she hold? It's not a snake now,
fur on a giant dark shape towering,
and claws – a bear, grinning and growling –
   'I must hold on, he said, he said.'

O what is she holding? Not a bear,
short hair in her fingers, antlers slashing,
sharp hooves – a stag, twisting and thrashing –
   'I must hold on, he said, he said.'

Hold what in her hands? Not a deer but dead
and heavy and hard and harsh as iron
but a red-hot bar of red-hot iron –
   'I must hold on, he said, he said.'

What's in her hand? Not the weight of iron,
small in her palm and flames that flicker –
a coal from the fire but cannot burn her –
    'Tam Lin, I'll win!' she said, she said.

She has thrown the coal into the well-water.
The shape of a man she has covered over.
    What of the terrors of the night?
He is under her green mantle, wrapped tight.

Then she heard the Queen of Elfland speak
    from a broom-bush close by:
'Shame on her ugly ill-fared face
    and an ill death may she die,
for she's taken the best and bonniest knight
    of all my company!

'O had I known this morning
    Tam Lin would be gone,
I'd have taken out his heart of flesh,
    given him a heart of stone.

'The look of his eyes this evening,
    O had I understood,
I'd have taken out his two grey eyes,
    given him eyes of wood.

'And had I learned last night Tam Lin
    the lesson I've learned now,
seven payments I'd have made to Hell
    before I let you go!'

The Queen of Elfland cursed and cried
    but her rage was vain.
Janet stood fast at Miles Cross,
    and she married Tam Lin.

The Old Woman and the Sandwiches

I met a wizened wood-woman
    Who begged a crumb of me.
Four sandwiches of ham I had:
    I gave her three.

'Bless you, thank you, kindly miss,
    Shall be rewarded well –
Three everlasting gifts, whose value
    None can tell.'

'Three wishes?' out I cried in glee –
    'No, gifts you may not choose:
A flea and gnat to bite your back
    And gravel in your shoes.'

Rowan Child

My green-haired rowan child,
last year you barely reached my knee.
This July, like a human nine-year-old,
you're big enough to see over the fence –
have you been watching like me
next door's new kittens totter and pounce?

A tiny flock of greenfly
huddles where the wind sways
the leaflets at your crown.
They've curled them right over –
it's a fair climb for their shepherd-ants
to this year's high pasture.
I can see one glob of cuckoo spit
and, down near the ground, a spider
no bigger than an apple-pip
who's hung out a flimsy net
like the ghost of a biscuit –
to think one day I'll be looking up at the sky
between your fingers!

When is your childhood over?
The spring your quiet hands show me
your first white catch of stars –
whose light may die,
but summer's slow magic I know
will set in their place
red swarms of blood-bright beads
like seeds of flame –
O will it be next year, or the year after?
And when the birds come,
shall I make them necklaces of them?
Shall we hold your birthday then?
Strange child, I'm only teasing,
I know you can't answer.

Writing this at my desk now,
I've my back to the open door
where you stand, like a guard.
Little tree, if the old belief
was true, that you could scare away
fairies and witches, bad thoughts, unkind wishes,
keep our house safe – O let no evil through.

The Trees Dance

Forest-father, mighty Oak:
On my back the lightning-stroke

Spear-maker, Ash-tree:
Safely cross the raging sea

Black-eyed Elder, crooked-arm:
Break me and you'll come to harm

Dark Yew, poison-cup:
Keep the ghosts from rising up

Summer's herald, Hawthorn, May:
Home of the fairies, keep away

Cry-a-leaf, the bitter Willow:
Where you walk at night I follow

Slender Hazel, water-hound:
In my nutshell wisdom found

Birch the dancer, best broom:
Sweep the evil from your room

Fair Apple, fire's sweet wood:
Dreams of power and poets' food

Winter-shiner, Holly the king:
Good cheer to the cold I bring

Rowan the guard, berry-red:
Fairies fear and witches dread

Souvenir from Weston-Super-Mare

Moving in a bunch like creeping hands
   the donkeys, prised from their hay,
cross the day's backdrop again; cloud, tide, mud
   cement the scene grey.

I scoop away. I build. I mould – the oil's
   good for adhesion. There, that
can do for the necessary moat,
   and look! *A sand-cat!*

Ears, nose, paws straight from Egypt. And still
   ten minutes before the bus.
We look back from the top of the wall.
   Long drawn out after us

a family comes breasting the wind –
   it'll be right in their track.
The boy spots it first, running ahead.
   He goes running back

to fetch the others. They cluster and point,
   looking up and down the strand
before the wind detaches them again.
   He waits. Their backs turned,

he drops to his knees, he strokes the sand fur.
   Come on – five past the bus leaves!
Dodging the weaving cars we race the station
   clock's hands light as thieves.

A Friend for the Wind

This is a story from long ago,
from the land of mountains and lakes that lies
near the top of the world, under the Northern skies,
bright as jewels in the sun, blue and white
in the long winter night.
But there were no creatures then.
It was an empty land.

The forests rustled, rivers chattered,
rocks and stones clacked and clattered,
ice creaked, snow flopped down from the trees –
and all the time, O with no ease,
over and through,
the wind flew.

And Wind howled,
      because he was sad
            because he was lonely
                 because he was
                             invisible.

'O you in your sure places, all of you,
black, white and grey, brown, green and blue,
snug in your homes I can only whirl over and through –
if only I had one special friend everyone could see,
to travel with, then – then you'd not forget me! . . .'

'There he goes again, poor old Wind,
howling for a friend –
he makes me shiver,' grumbled River.

'I know!' said Old Rock. 'Let's make him one!
Why not? See if we can –
we've got time before he comes back.'

'How do we begin?' asked Grass
who was leant over, listening.
'I don't mind giving a tussock or two – '

'You can have my tawny colours then,'
called Sandbank, ' – instead of green!'

'I'll ripple it into a pattern for you,'
River said. 'There, that looks fine.'

'Here's a slice of my broad back
to put it on,' said Old Rock.
'This is good!'

Then Fir Tree whispered from the wood,
'How about this overgrown bough of mine?
Just feel its thick needles!
And if you need something more,
there ought to be four good sticks near my feet
that broke off in a storm –
I'll see if I can find them . . .'

'Have me!' chirped a lumpy Stone,
narrowed at one end – like a kind of rough cone.
'Where shall I sit? This is fun!
Better cover me too, Grass – come on!'

'What does it look like?'
they called up to Great Mountain.
'How are we doing?'

But she said:
'Don't wake me now,
I like to sleep when the Wind's off howling somewhere else.'

No one saw Frost creeping up through the moss
till he jumped out shouting 'Hey, catch!'
and chucked them a bunch of little icicles –
'Any use?'

'Thanks,' said Blueberry Bush.
'I've some bare twigs I can fix them along first,
before they get lost –
but please go away Frost,
you're making my teeth chatter . . .'

Then a deep voice boomed in their ears.
It was Cave.
'I've a spare pair
of miniature doorways in here.
Pointed at the top. Like flames.
Rather smart. Too small
to be much good to me.
Would you like them?'

And Riverbed said,
'You've *just* reminded me
there's a couple of pale gold pebbles
somewhere among my treasures
that match perfectly –
I'll *just* look them out.'

Never was there such a bustle and fuss
in the Northland
as the word went round:
We're making a friend for the Wind!
Nothing wanted to be left out.
But with this, that and everything
to fashion and fit,
they were far too busy to notice
Night rolling in from the east –
who said nothing at all,
but poured her bowl
of darkness
over them and their workshop
and they had to stop.

By and by, the Sun
came striding over Great Mountain.
'Whatever's this?
What have you all been doing?
I can see
something like a
pepper-coloured
rug-covered
table,
with a soft
brush hanging off one end,
and a kind of fat
shield at the other, with two model
tepees on the top of it and a couple of shiny
coins stuck half-way down,
and –

oh you'll have to tell me,
I can't guess!'

'We're trying to make a special
friend for the Wind,'
Old Rock explained.
'He howls so, he's so lonely.
But it's turned out a bit small and patchy.'

'I'll help,'
the Sun smiled,
and she scooped a handful of heat
right out of her heart
and lobbed it down to them.

'What's that?' they cried.

'Oh,' she said, 'life. You'll see.
'But first,
Strange New Thing
what shall we call you?

Wind's Own Loyal Friend
Warding Off Loneliness Forever –
Wander Our Land Fearlessly
Watch Over Life Fiercely
now
Welcome, O Light-Footed
Wild One – Live Free!

WOLF is your name, and WOLF you shall be!'

Then Wolf began
stretching himself.
He shook his thick fur coat
from neck to tail-tip
flapping his wide paws
one by one –
and looking up as he yawned
Wolf caught the Sun's smile
in his great jaws,
and Wolf grinned.

'O yes, welcome Wolf!' they cried. 'You'll
be a friend to us all!'

'You'll run on and on like me –
and anywhere!' said River.

All Forest's Fir Trees murmured:
'You can weave our shadows together!'

'You'll kill sharp as I can!'
called bright Frost from the shade of a hollow.

'You can curl up in a corner with us
whenever you like,' chorused Old Rock and Cave below.

And then, coming from far off across the land,
they heard a howl.
They had quite forgotten the lonely Wind.

'What shall we do? We needn't tell him! He won't know!
Let's keep Wolf for ourselves! Sh, don't say a word!
We'll try and make something else for him tomorrow – '

They didn't think he could hear them.
Of course, they couldn't see
how he hid his head in his hands, he was so miserable,
though they heard well enough
the terrible sadness in his howling.

Wolf heard it too.
Wolf heard everything.
He gathered his new long legs
to spring
with a great leap
on top of Old Rock,
and there,
nose to the Wind,
he stretched his warm throat like a fur horn
and joined in.

The song of his howl
rose and fell on the air
like the burst of a slow firework
and all its hanging flowers.

The Sun blinked.
A shiver ran
right the way down Great Mountain's spine –
she shook off sleep like a cloud
and shone.
Frost froze quite still
and after a while
the stars themselves came solemnly to their doors
to listen.

As for the Wind, he lay down to rest,
happy at last.

Was that the end?
No. From the new silence
life with a million surprises
began to break out all over the wilderness.
Flying it came, and running,
it swam, ambled, scuttered and crept.
And from that day, wherever the Wind
went whooping and swooping,
Wolf hunted and played and slept –
among the close trees, across the barrens,
by the cold lakes, rocks and rivers –
and everywhere gave Wolf a home,
for Wolf was a special friend
to all of them.

Long, long after – hundreds of years –
people came from across the sea,
looked at the wild wide land
and said it was theirs.

Whose?

Theirs – they said so.
They were ready to fight to make it so.
And when they saw Wolf,
Wolf's eyes in the night,
Wolf-tracks in the snow,
they saw danger, they saw an enemy.
Wolf would have to go.

So these were their gifts: traps, bullets, poisoned bait –
well-picked for a Worthless Outcast Lawless Fiend –

O but they trembled at the music in the Wind,
they trembled at the music in the Wind.

A Good Idea for Wintry Weather

At breakfast in the dark I pop
my dad's hat over the teapot
so that his head shall be hot
though the full buses pass his stop.

The Guarded Treasure

A story from Herefordshire

Penyard castle's a heap of stones,
Roofless walls where the wind moans,

Nettles and thorns on the broken stair,
And nobody knows what's hidden there.

Down in the vaults there's an iron door
Whoever opens shall want no more:

Open the door, there's barrels of gold
Whoever finds, beware, be bold:

Barrels of gold and barrels of treasure
Whoever takes – shall be rich for ever.

'Gold and treasure? A hoard of the stuff?
I'll be rich for ever – I'm bold enough!

'Go round up the oxen, see them fed!
Ten good beasts he has, white and red,

To yoke to the waggon, two by two,
And he fastened their yokes with pins of yew;

And a stick to drive them hard as he could –
The stick was carved from rowan wood.

Weary the road and the day, and late
When he brought his waggon through Penyard gate.

Nobody there and none to see,
But a jackdaw, perched on an elder tree.

Corner by corner he searched the stones,
But all he found was rubble and bones,

Nettles and thorns, and the wind blew cold.
'I'm a fool to believe in barrels of gold!'

Dark lay the shadows on wall and sill,
But behind the elder was darker still.

He has torn the tree right out of the ground,
And there the iron door he found.

No lock nor bolt to hold it tight
But it moved not one hairsbreadth for all his might.

He has harnessed his oxen to the ring:
'Now pull that door till you make it spring!'

He shouted them on, he beat them sore –
Till at last, by a little, they moved the door.

He squints at the dark through the narrow crack:
Barrel on barrel, stack by stack –

And perched on the top where the walls close in,
A bead-eyed jackdaw, watching him.

'One more pull, and I'm rich for ever!'
The oxen strain, the oxen stagger

And pull – and a roar like a clap of thunder
Bursts the air, the earth quakes under,

Wings with the dark go rushing past:
With a hollow crash the door slams fast.

And out of the walls a thin voice cried:
What earth has hidden, the earth shall hide:

And but for a yoke with a yew-tree pin
All your cattle had been pulled in

And but for a stick of rowan wood
You had been hauled from the world for good.

Penyard castle's a heap of stones,
Roofless walls where the wind moans,

Nettles and thorns on the broken stair,
And one man alive knows what lies there:

An iron door to untold treasure –
Whoever enters is lost for ever.

'Better than all your gold to me
The yew tree, and the rowan tree!'

A Dance of Moths

Mother Shipton,
the Red-necked Footman,
the Drinker, the Brick
and the Snout
pressed the close sides
of their chrysalids:
time to climb out.

Brightline Brown Eye,
Pretty Chalk Carpet,
the Ghost, the Old Lady,
the Shark:
brushing the dew
with throbbing wings,
they danced in the dark.

Rosy Rustic,
the Garden Tiger,
Dark Arches, the Flame
and the Mouse:
out in the cool air
they saw the light,
and came to my house.

Source Books

The Dragonfly: Philip S. Corbet, Cynthia Longfield and N. W. Moore, *Dragonflies,* (Collins, 1960) (New Naturalist series) Enid Blyton, *Nature Readers,* (Macmillan, 1945-6)

The Story of Arachne: Ovid, *The Metamorphoses,* trans. Mary M. Innes, (Penguin Books, 1955) Book VI

The Story of Canobie Dick: W. W. Gibbings, 'Canobie Dick and Thomas of Ercildoun' from *Folk Lore and Legends, Scotland,* (1889) as retold in *A Dictionary of British Folk Tales in the English Language, Part B: Folk Legends,* Katharine M. Briggs, (Routledge & Kegan Paul, 1971)

The Journey of Hanuman: *The Ramayana* (from the Bengali text), trans. Shudha Mazumdar, (Orient Longman, 1974)
The Ramayana of Valmiki (Banaras version), trans. Makhan Lal Sen, (Munshiram Mancharlal Publrs, New Delhi, 1976)
Hanuman, Amar Chitra Katha No 19, *Tales of Hanuman,* Bumper Issue No 1, (comic version), (IBH Publrs Pvt Ltd, Bombay, c.1970, 1989 – Eng. edn.)
Elizabeth Seeger, *The Ramayana* (told for children), (Dent, 1975)

In the Bee-Factory: Maurice Maeterlinck, *The Life of the Bee,* trans. Alfred Suto, (Mentor Books, 1954)

The Ballad of the Great Bear: Ovid, *The Metamorphoses,* trans. Mary M. Innes, (Penguin Books, 1955) Book II

Orion the Hunter: Robert Graves, *The Greek Myths,* (Penguin Books, 1955) Vol. I
Richard Hinckley Allen, *Star Names, Their Lore and Meaning,* (Dover, 1963)

Tam Lin: A. Quiller-Couch, *The Oxford Book of Ballads,* (OUP, 1910)
J. Kinsley, *The Oxford Book of Ballads,* (OUP, 1969)

The Trees Dance: Robert Graves, *The White Goddess,* (Faber, 1961)
Geoffrey Grigson, *The Englishman's Flora,* (Paladin, 1975)

The Guarded Treasure: Geoffrey Grigson, *The Englishman's Flora,* (Paladin, 1975)

A Dance of Moths, Caterpillar-Keeper: John Burton, *The Oxford Book of Insects,* (OUP, 1968)

Acknowledgements

The following poems were originally commissioned by Paddy Bechely for the BBC Schools Radio series, *Stories & Rhymes* (becoming *Pictures in Your Mind* in 1983), and first broadcast in the programmes given below:

A Dance of Moths – *Into the Air*, 1974;   A Friend for the Wind – *A Friend for the Wind*, 1984;   All Change! – *The First Spider's Web*, 1977;   Ant Town – *Maze Dances*, 1981;   Black Dot – *Into the Air*, 1974;   Caterpillar-Keeper – *Out of the Dark*, 1974;   Flying to India – *Flying to India*, 1980;   In the Bee-Factory – *Out of the Dark*, 1974;   Like a Maze – *Maze Dances*, 1981;   Orion the Hunter – *Stories of the Stars*, 1984;   Rowan Child – *Tree Magic*, 1985;   Something for a Blue-bottle – *Into the Air*, 1974; Talk About Caves – *The Secrets of Caves*, 1983;   Tam Lin – *Tam Lin*, 1979;   The Ballad of the Great Bear – *Stories of the Stars*, 1984;   The Dragonfly – *Into the Air*, 1974;   The Dream of the Cabbage Caterpillars – *Out of the Dark*, 1974;   The Guarded Treasure – *Tree Magic*, 1985;   The Journey of Hanuman (1-10) – *The Journey of the Monkey God*, 1979;   The Key to the Maze – *Maze Dances*, 1981;   The Story of Arachne – *The First Spider's Web*, 1977;   The Story of Canobie Dick – *The Secrets of Caves*, 1983;   The Trees Dance – *Tree Magic*, 1985.

All the above poems were first published in the accompanying pupils' pamphlets; A Rhyme for Autumn was first published in 'The Fair Forest' (1985), the pamphlet accompanying the programme *Tree Magic*. The Journey of Hanuman (11-18) was first broadcast in the BBC Schools Radio *Contact* series, 1989.

The Tale of the Estuary and the Hedge and Outside In first appeared in *A Stained Glass Raree Show* (Allison & Busby, 1967); Rotting Song and The Old Woman and the Sandwiches in *Plain Clothes* (Allison & Busby, 1971); and Midsummer Stars in *Necessity* (Slow Dancer Press, 1988). A Good Idea for Wintry Weather was first published in *A Very First Poetry Book* (OUP, 1984). Thanks are also due to the editors of the magazines *Poor. Old. Tired. Horse.*, *Slow Dancer*, and *Smoke* in which the remaining poems first appeared.